D1577457

FOR THE BEST
TEACHER
IN THE
WORLD

summersdale

FOR THE BEST TEACHER IN THE WORLD

Summersdale Publishers Ltd
46 West Street
Chichester
West Sussex
PO19 1RP
UK

www.summersdale.com

Printed and bound in the Czech Republic

ISBN: 978-1-84953-619-6

Substantial discounts on bulk quantities of Summersdale books are available to corporations, professional associations and other organisations. For details contact Nicky Douglas by telephone: +44 (0) 1243 756902, fax: +44 (0) 1243 786300 or email: nicky@summersdale.com

TO...

FROM...

THE ART OF TEACHING IS THE ART OF ASSISTING DISCOVERY.

Mark Van Doren

THE BEST TEACHERS
TEACH FROM THE HEART,
NOT FROM THE BOOK.

Anonymous

I BELIEVE EFFECTIVE
LEADERS ARE, FIRST
AND FOREMOST, GOOD
TEACHERS.

John Wooden

BEFORE ANY
GREAT THINGS ARE
ACCOMPLISHED, A
MEMORABLE CHANGE
MUST BE MADE IN THE
SYSTEM OF EDUCATION...
TO RAISE THE LOWER
RANKS OF SOCIETY
NEARER TO THE HIGHER.

John Adams

I CANNOT TEACH
ANYBODY ANYTHING,
I CAN ONLY MAKE
THEM THINK.

Socrates

IF YOU ARE PLANNING
FOR A YEAR, SOW RICE;
IF YOU ARE PLANNING
FOR A DECADE, PLANT
TREES; IF YOU ARE
PLANNING FOR A
LIFETIME, EDUCATE
PEOPLE.

Chinese proverb

WHAT SCULPTURE IS TO
A BLOCK OF MARBLE,
EDUCATION IS TO A
HUMAN SOUL.

Joseph Addison

THE REAL OBJECT OF
EDUCATION IS TO GIVE
CHILDREN RESOURCES
THAT WILL ENDURE AS
LONG AS LIFE ENDURES.

Sydney Smith

WHEN YOU WANT TO
BUILD A SHIP, DO NOT
BEGIN BY GATHERING
WOOD, CUTTING BOARDS,
AND DISTRIBUTING
WORK, BUT RATHER
AWAKEN WITHIN MEN
THE DESIRE FOR THE
VAST AND ENDLESS SEA.

Antoine de Saint-Exupéry

THANK YOU FOR EVERYTHING!

EDUCATION BREEDS
CONFIDENCE. CONFIDENCE
BREEDS HOPE. HOPE
BREEDS PEACE.

Confucius

EVERY CHILD DESERVES
A CHAMPION — AN ADULT
WHO WILL NEVER GIVE
UP ON THEM.

Rita Pierson

IF SOMEONE IS GOING DOWN THE WRONG ROAD, HE DOESN'T NEED MOTIVATION TO SPEED HIM UP. WHAT HE NEEDS IS EDUCATION TO TURN HIM AROUND.

Jim Rohn

TELL ME AND I FORGET.
TEACH ME AND I
REMEMBER. INVOLVE ME
AND I LEARN.

Benjamin Franklin

THE OBJECT OF
TEACHING A CHILD IS
TO ENABLE HIM TO GET
ALONG WITHOUT HIS
TEACHER.

Elbert Hubbard

EDUCATION IS NOT
PREPARATION FOR LIFE;
EDUCATION IS LIFE
ITSELF.

John Dewey

ONE'S MIND, ONCE
STRETCHED BY A NEW
IDEA, NEVER REGAINS ITS
ORIGINAL DIMENSIONS.

Oliver Wendell Holmes Jr

THE FUTURE CANNOT
BE PREDICTED, BUT
FUTURES CAN BE
INVENTED.

Dennis Gabor

THE FUNCTION OF
EDUCATION... IS TO
TEACH ONE TO THINK
INTENSIVELY AND TO
THINK CRITICALLY.

Martin Luther King Jr

THE SECRET OF TEACHING
IS TO APPEAR TO HAVE
KNOWN ALL YOUR LIFE
WHAT YOU JUST LEARNED
THIS MORNING.

Anonymous

THANK YOU FOR
PUSHING ME TO
BE THE BEST
I CAN BE

CHILDREN MUST BE
TAUGHT HOW TO THINK,
NOT WHAT TO THINK.

Margaret Mead

THE PRINCIPAL GOAL
OF EDUCATION... SHOULD
BE CREATING MEN
AND WOMEN WHO ARE
CAPABLE OF DOING
NEW THINGS.

Jean Piaget

A TEACHER IS A COMPASS
THAT ACTIVATES THE
MAGNETS OF CURIOSITY,
KNOWLEDGE AND WISDOM
IN THE PUPILS.

Ever Garrison

WE OFTEN TAKE FOR
GRANTED THE VERY
THINGS THAT MOST
DESERVE OUR GRATITUDE.

Cynthia Ozick

IDEAL TEACHERS
ARE THOSE WHO USE
THEMSELVES AS BRIDGES
OVER WHICH THEY
INVITE THEIR STUDENTS
TO CROSS.

Nikos Kazantzakis

EDUCATION IS WHAT
SURVIVES WHEN WHAT
HAS BEEN LEARNED HAS
BEEN FORGOTTEN.

B. F. Skinner

THE VERY SPRING
AND ROOT OF HONESTY
AND VIRTUE LIE IN
GOOD EDUCATION.

Plutarch

WHEN YOU LEARN, TEACH. WHEN YOU GET, GIVE.

Maya Angelou

A TRULY SPECIAL
TEACHER IS VERY WISE,
AND SEES TOMORROW IN
EVERY CHILD'S EYES.

Anonymous

I AM NOT A TEACHER, BUT AN AWAKENER.

Robert Frost

SHALL I TELL YOU THE
SECRET OF THE TRUE
SCHOLAR? IT IS THIS:
EVERY MAN I MEET IS
MY MASTER IN SOME
POINT, AND IN THAT I
LEARN OF HIM.

Ralph Waldo Emerson

STUDY AS IF YOU WERE
TO LIVE FOREVER.

Mahatma Gandhi

YOU ARE AN INSPIRATION!

WHAT WE LEARN WITH PLEASURE, WE NEVER FORGET.

Alfred Mercier

GOOD TEACHING IS ONE-
FOURTH PREPARATION
AND THREE-FOURTHS
THEATRE.

Gail Godwin

TEACHERS TOUCH
THE FUTURE.

Carol Milson

THE MIND IS NOT A
VESSEL THAT NEEDS
FILLING, BUT WOOD THAT
NEEDS IGNITING.

Plutarch

THE BEAUTIFUL THING
ABOUT LEARNING IS
THAT NO ONE CAN TAKE
IT AWAY FROM YOU.

B. B. King

BETTER THAN A THOUSAND DAYS OF DILIGENT STUDY IS ONE DAY WITH A GREAT TEACHER.

Japanese proverb

LOGIC WILL GET
YOU FROM A TO B.
IMAGINATION WILL TAKE
YOU EVERYWHERE.

Albert Einstein

EDUCATION IS THE MOST
POWERFUL WEAPON
WHICH YOU CAN USE TO
CHANGE THE WORLD.

Nelson Mandela

TO TEACH IS TO LEARN TWICE OVER.

Joseph Joubert

LAUGHTER IS TIMELESS.
IMAGINATION HAS NO
AGE. AND DREAMS
ARE FOREVER.

Walt Disney

A TEACHER AFFECTS
ETERNITY; HE CAN
NEVER TELL WHERE HIS
INFLUENCE STOPS.

Henry Adams

THE HARDEST
THING TO TEACH IS
HOW TO CARE.

Anonymous

YOU MAKE
LEARNING FUN!

EACH OF US HAS A FIRE
IN OUR HEARTS FOR
SOMETHING. IT'S OUR
GOAL IN LIFE TO FIND IT
AND KEEP IT LIT.

Mary Lou Retton

EVERY TRUTH HAS FOUR
CORNERS: AS A TEACHER
I GIVE YOU ONE CORNER,
AND IT IS FOR YOU TO
FIND THE OTHER THREE.

Confucius

THE MORE THAT YOU
READ, THE MORE
THINGS YOU WILL
KNOW. THE MORE THAT
YOU LEARN, THE MORE
PLACES YOU'LL GO.

Dr Seuss

IF YOU CAN TEACH
[A STUDENT] TO LEARN
BY CREATING CURIOSITY,
HE WILL CONTINUE THE
LEARNING PROCESS AS
LONG AS HE LIVES.

Clay P. Bedford

THE AIM OF EDUCATION
SHOULD BE TO TEACH US
RATHER HOW TO THINK,
THAN WHAT TO THINK.

James Beattie

DO NOT CONFINE YOUR CHILDREN TO YOUR OWN LEARNING, FOR THEY WERE BORN IN ANOTHER TIME.

Hebrew proverb

WHO DARES TO TEACH MUST NEVER CEASE TO LEARN.

John Cotton Dana

TEACHERS SHOULD BE THE HIGHEST PAID EMPLOYEES ON EARTH.

Anonymous

ONCE YOU HAVE
LEARNED HOW TO ASK
QUESTIONS — RELEVANT
AND APPROPRIATE AND
SUBSTANTIAL QUESTIONS
— YOU HAVE LEARNED
HOW TO LEARN.

Neil Postman and
Charles Weingartner

I'M NOT AFRAID OF
STORMS, FOR I'M
LEARNING HOW TO
SAIL MY SHIP.

Louisa May Alcott

WHEN YOU TEACH YOUR SON, YOU TEACH YOUR SON'S SON.

The Talmud

BY TEACHING, WE LEARN.

Latin proverb

YOU ALWAYS
KNOW THE
ANSWER

A TRUE TEACHER
SHOULD PENETRATE TO
WHATEVER IS VITAL IN
HIS PUPIL, AND DEVELOP
THAT BY THE LIGHT
AND HEAT OF HIS OWN
INTELLIGENCE.

Edwin Percy Whipple

TEACHERS WHO INSPIRE
REALISE THERE WILL
ALWAYS BE BLOCKS
IN THE ROAD AHEAD
OF US. THEY WILL BE
STUMBLING BLOCKS OR
STEPPING STONES; IT ALL
DEPENDS ON HOW WE
USE THEM.

Anonymous

A TEACHER'S PURPOSE IS NOT TO CREATE STUDENTS IN HIS OWN IMAGE, BUT TO DEVELOP STUDENTS WHO CAN CREATE THEIR OWN IMAGE.

Anonymous

THE AVERAGE TEACHER
EXPLAINS COMPLEXITY;
THE GIFTED TEACHER
REVEALS SIMPLICITY.

Robert Brault

WHAT NOBLER
EMPLOYMENT, OR MORE
VALUABLE TO THE STATE,
THAN THAT OF THE MAN
WHO INSTRUCTS THE
RISING GENERATION.

Cicero

THE IMPORTANT THING
IS NOT SO MUCH THAT
EVERY CHILD SHOULD BE
TAUGHT, AS THAT EVERY
CHILD SHOULD BE GIVEN
THE WISH TO LEARN.

John Lubbock

THOSE WHO EDUCATE
CHILDREN WELL ARE
MORE TO BE HONOURED
THAN PARENTS, FOR
THESE ONLY GAVE LIFE,
THOSE THE ART OF
LIVING WELL.

Aristotle

BY LEARNING YOU WILL TEACH; BY TEACHING YOU WILL UNDERSTAND.

Latin proverb

EDUCATION IS THE MOTHER OF LEADERSHIP.

Wendell Willkie

TEACHING IS LEAVING
A VESTIGE OF ONE SELF
IN THE DEVELOPMENT
OF ANOTHER.

Eugene P. Bertin

THE MEDIOCRE TEACHER
TELLS. THE GOOD
TEACHER EXPLAINS.
THE SUPERIOR TEACHER
DEMONSTRATES. THE
GREAT TEACHER
INSPIRES.

William Arthur Ward

WHAT OFFICE IS THERE
WHICH INVOLVES
MORE RESPONSIBILITY,
WHICH REQUIRES
MORE QUALIFICATIONS,
AND WHICH OUGHT,
THEREFORE, TO BE MORE
HONOURABLE THAN
TEACHING?

Harriet Martineau

YOU HELPED
ME TO ENJOY
SCHOOL

SELDOM EVER WAS ANY
KNOWLEDGE GIVEN TO
KEEP, BUT TO IMPART;
THE GRACE OF THIS
RICH JEWEL IS LOST IN
CONCEALMENT.

Joseph Hall

IF YOU WOULD
THOROUGHLY KNOW
ANYTHING, TEACH IT
TO OTHERS.

Tryon Edwards

THE DREAM BEGINS
WITH A TEACHER WHO
BELIEVES IN YOU, WHO
TUGS AND PUSHES AND
LEADS YOU TO THE
NEXT PLATEAU.

Dan Rather

TEACHING SHOULD
BE FULL OF IDEAS
INSTEAD OF STUFFED
WITH FACTS.

Anonymous

WE CANNOT HOLD
A TORCH TO LIGHT
ANOTHER'S PATH
WITHOUT BRIGHTENING
OUR OWN.

Ben Sweetland

SOMEWHERE, SOMETHING
INCREDIBLE IS WAITING
TO BE KNOWN.

Carl Sagan

THE BEST TEACHER IS ONE WHO SUGGESTS RATHER THAN DOGMATISES, AND INSPIRES HIS LISTENER WITH THE WISH TO TEACH HIMSELF.

Edward Bulwer-Lytton

NATURAL ABILITY
IS BY FAR THE BEST,
BUT MANY MEN HAVE
SUCCEEDED IN WINNING
HIGH RENOWN BY SKILL
THAT IS THE FRUIT
OF TEACHING.

Pindar

IT IS THE SUPREME
ART OF THE TEACHER
TO AWAKEN JOY IN
CREATIVE EXPRESSION
AND KNOWLEDGE.

Albert Einstein

YOU CANNOT TEACH A
MAN ANYTHING; YOU CAN
ONLY HELP HIM TO FIND
IT WITHIN HIMSELF.

Galileo

WHAT THE TEACHER IS,
IS MORE IMPORTANT
THAN WHAT HE TEACHES.

Karl Menninger

ONE LOOKS BACK WITH
APPRECIATION TO THE
BRILLIANT TEACHERS,
BUT WITH GRATITUDE
TO THOSE WHO TOUCHED
OUR HUMAN FEELINGS.

Carl Jung

YOU ARE MY
FAVOURITE
TEACHER

THE MOST EFFECTIVE
TEACHER WILL
ALWAYS BE BIASED,
FOR THE CHIEF
FORCE IN TEACHING
IS CONFIDENCE AND
ENTHUSIASM.

Joyce Cary

IT IS A LUXURY TO
LEARN; BUT THE LUXURY
OF LEARNING IS NOT TO
BE COMPARED WITH THE
LUXURY OF TEACHING.

Roswell Dwight Hitchcock

EDUCATION IS THE
GUARDIAN GENIUS OF
DEMOCRACY. IT IS THE
ONLY DICTATOR THAT
FREE MEN RECOGNISE,
AND THE ONLY RULER
THAT FREE MEN
REQUIRE.

Mirabeau B. Lamar

THE TRUE AIM OF
EVERYONE WHO
ASPIRES TO BE A
TEACHER SHOULD BE,
NOT TO IMPART HIS
OWN OPINIONS, BUT TO
KINDLE MINDS.

Frederick William Robertson

TO ME, EDUCATION IS A
LEADING OUT OF WHAT IS
ALREADY THERE IN THE
PUPIL'S SOUL.

Muriel Spark

A GOOD TEACHER
IS A MASTER OF
SIMPLIFICATION AND AN
ENEMY OF SIMPLISM.

Louis A. Berman

NINE-TENTHS OF EDUCATION IS ENCOURAGEMENT.

Anatole France

WHATEVER YOU WANT TO TEACH, BE BRIEF.

Horace

HE THAT TEACHES US
ANYTHING WHICH WE
KNEW NOT BEFORE IS
UNDOUBTEDLY TO BE
REVERENCED AS
A MASTER.

Samuel Johnson

TEACHERS WHO INSPIRE
KNOW THAT TEACHING
IS LIKE CULTIVATING A
GARDEN, AND THOSE WHO
WOULD HAVE NOTHING
TO DO WITH THORNS
MUST NEVER ATTEMPT
TO GATHER FLOWERS.

Anonymous

THE TASK OF THE
EXCELLENT TEACHER
IS TO STIMULATE
'APPARENTLY ORDINARY'
PEOPLE TO UNUSUAL
EFFORT.

K. Patricia Cross

EDUCATION IS THE
MOVEMENT FROM
DARKNESS TO LIGHT.

Allan Bloom

YOU ARE
ALWAYS FAIR

IF YOU HAVE
KNOWLEDGE, LET
OTHERS LIGHT THEIR
CANDLES WITH IT.

Margaret Fuller

I HEAR AND I FORGET.
I SEE AND I REMEMBER.
I DO AND I UNDERSTAND.

Chinese proverb

BE CAREFUL TO LEAVE
YOUR SONS WELL
INSTRUCTED RATHER
THAN RICH, FOR
THE HOPES OF THE
INSTRUCTED ARE BETTER
THAN THE WEALTH OF
THE IGNORANT.

Epictetus

FINALLY, EDUCATION
ALONE CAN CONDUCT US
TO THAT ENJOYMENT
WHICH IS, AT ONCE,
BEST IN QUALITY AND
INFINITE IN QUANTITY.

Horace Mann

I AM INDEBTED TO MY
FATHER FOR LIVING,
BUT TO MY TEACHER
FOR LIVING WELL.

Alexander the Great

TO KNOW HOW TO
SUGGEST IS THE GREAT
ART OF TEACHING.

Henri-Frédéric Amiel

EDUCATION IS THE TRANSMISSION OF CIVILISATION.

Will Durant

A SCHOOLMASTER
SHOULD HAVE AN
ATMOSPHERE OF AWE,
AND WALK WONDERINGLY,
AS IF HE WAS AMAZED
AT BEING HIMSELF.

Walter Bagehot

A MASTER CAN TELL
YOU WHAT HE EXPECTS
OF YOU. A TEACHER,
THOUGH, AWAKENS YOUR
OWN EXPECTATIONS.

Patricia Neal

EDUCATION MAKES A
PEOPLE EASY TO LEAD,
BUT DIFFICULT TO DRIVE;
EASY TO GOVERN, BUT
IMPOSSIBLE TO ENSLAVE.

Henry Brougham

I HAVE LEARNED SO MUCH FROM YOU

OUR PROGRESS AS
A NATION CAN BE NO
SWIFTER THAN OUR
PROGRESS IN EDUCATION.

John F. Kennedy

EDUCATION IS SIMPLY
THE SOUL OF A SOCIETY
AS IT PASSES FROM
ONE GENERATION
TO ANOTHER.

G. K. Chesterton

INSTRUCTION ENDS IN
THE SCHOOLROOM, BUT
EDUCATION ENDS ONLY
WITH LIFE.

Frederick William Robertson

A PART OF THE FUNCTION OF EDUCATION TO HELP US ESCAPE... FROM THE INTELLECTUAL AND EMOTIONAL LIMITATIONS OF OUR TIME.

T. S. Eliot

WHATEVER IS GOOD
TO KNOW IS DIFFICULT
TO LEARN.

Greek proverb

THE ESSENCE OF TEACHING IS TO MAKE LEARNING CONTAGIOUS, TO HAVE ONE IDEA SPARK ANOTHER.

Marva Collins

EDUCATION IS THE
ABILITY TO LISTEN
TO ALMOST ANYTHING
WITHOUT LOSING YOUR
TEMPER OR YOUR
SELF-CONFIDENCE.

Robert Frost

WHAT WE HAVE
LEARNED FROM OTHERS
BECOMES OUR OWN BY
REFLECTION.

Ralph Waldo Emerson

A TEACHER WHO IS
ATTEMPTING TO TEACH
WITHOUT INSPIRING THE
PUPIL WITH A DESIRE TO
LEARN IS HAMMERING
ON COLD IRON.

Horace Mann

THE BEST AND MOST
IMPORTANT PART OF
EVERY MAN'S EDUCATION
IS THAT WHICH HE
GIVES HIMSELF.

Edward Gibbon

EDUCATION IS THE KEY TO UNLOCK THE GOLDEN DOOR OF FREEDOM.

George Washington Carver

IT IS GREATER WORK
TO EDUCATE A CHILD, IN
THE TRUE AND LARGER
SENSE OF THE WORD,
THAN TO RULE A STATE.

William Ellery Channing

YOU TEACH ME
TO BE A BETTER
PERSON, NOT
JUST A BETTER
STUDENT

EDUCATION IS THE APPRENTICESHIP OF LIFE.

Robert Aris Willmott

LEARNING IS THE ONLY
THING THE MIND NEVER
EXHAUSTS, NEVER
FEARS, AND NEVER
REGRETS.

Leonardo da Vinci

EDUCATION IS MORE
THAN A LUXURY; IT IS
A RESPONSIBILITY THAT
SOCIETY OWES TO ITSELF.

Robin Cook

A GOOD TEACHER IS LIKE
A CANDLE — IT CONSUMES
ITSELF TO LIGHT THE
WAY FOR OTHERS.

Anonymous

THE TRUE TEACHER
DEFENDS HIS PUPILS
AGAINST HIS OWN
PERSONAL INFLUENCE...
HE GUIDES THEIR EYES
FROM HIMSELF TO THE
SPIRIT THAT QUICKENS
HIM. HE WILL HAVE
NO DISCIPLE.

Amos Bronson Alcott

LET US NEVER BE
BETRAYED INTO SAYING
WE HAVE FINISHED OUR
EDUCATION; BECAUSE
THAT WOULD MEAN WE
HAD STOPPED GROWING.

Julia Gulliver

TEACHING CREATES ALL OTHER PROFESSIONS.

Anonymous

CHARACTER IS A
WISH FOR A PERFECT
EDUCATION.

Novalis

THE ULTIMATE GOAL
OF THE EDUCATIONAL
SYSTEM IS TO SHIFT TO
THE INDIVIDUAL THE
BURDEN OF PURSUING
HIS OWN EDUCATION.

John W. Gardner

NEXT IN IMPORTANCE
TO FREEDOM AND
JUSTICE IS POPULAR
EDUCATION, WITHOUT
WHICH NEITHER
FREEDOM NOR JUSTICE
CAN BE PERMANENTLY
MAINTAINED.

James A. Garfield

EMERALDS AS WELL
AS GLASS WILL SHINE
WHEN THE LIGHT IS
SHED ON THEM.

Japanese proverb

TEACH THE CHILDREN! IT IS PAINTING IN FRESCO.

Ralph Waldo Emerson

YOU HELP
ME SEE MY
STRENGTHS

LEARNING IS LIKE
ROWING UPSTREAM:
NOT TO ADVANCE IS
TO DROP BACK.

Chinese proverb

EDUCATION SHOULD
BRING TO LIGHT
THE IDEAL OF
THE INDIVIDUAL.

Jean Paul

THERE ARE THREE
GOOD REASONS TO BE
A TEACHER — JUNE,
JULY AND AUGUST.

Anonymous

LOVE IS THE GREATEST
OF EDUCATORS.

Frances Sargent Osgood

THE GREATEST... SUCCESS
FOR A TEACHER IS TO
SAY, 'THE CHILDREN ARE
NOW WORKING AS IF I
DID NOT EXIST.'

Maria Montessori

EDUCATION'S PURPOSE
IS TO REPLACE AN
EMPTY MIND WITH
AN OPEN ONE.

Malcolm Forbes

EDUCATION IS
THE BEST PROVISION
FOR OLD AGE.

Aristotle

THE JOB OF AN
EDUCATOR IS TO
TEACH STUDENTS TO
SEE THE VITALITY
IN THEMSELVES.

Joseph Campbell

THE INSTINCT OF
CURIOSITY IS AT THE
BASE OF MANY OF
MAN'S MOST SPLENDID
ACHIEVEMENTS.

William McDougall

EDUCATION SHOULD
CONSIST OF... RAISING
THE INDIVIDUAL TO
A HIGHER LEVEL
OF AWARENESS,
UNDERSTANDING AND
KINSHIP WITH ALL
LIVING THINGS.

Anonymous

THE OBJECT OF EDUCATION
IS TO PREPARE THE YOUNG
TO EDUCATE THEMSELVES
THROUGHOUT THEIR LIVES.

Robert Maynard Hutchins

GOOD TEACHERS
MAKE THE BEST OF A
PUPIL'S MEANS; GREAT
TEACHERS FORESEE A
PUPIL'S ENDS.

Maria Callas

YOU ARE
ALWAYS SO
ENCOURAGING

TEACHING KIDS TO
COUNT IS FINE, BUT
TEACHING THEM WHAT
COUNTS IS BEST.

Bob Talbert

A TEACHER'S JOB IS
TO TAKE A BUNCH OF
LIVE WIRES AND SEE
THAT THEY ARE
WELL GROUNDED.

Anonymous

CREATIVITY IS...
THE ABILITY TO MAKE
CONNECTIONS, TO MAKE
ASSOCIATIONS, TO TURN
THINGS AROUND AND
EXPRESS THEM IN A
NEW WAY.

Tim Hansen

IF HE IS INDEED WISE
HE DOES NOT BID YOU
TO ENTER THE HOUSE
OF HIS WISDOM, BUT
RATHER LEADS YOU TO
THE THRESHOLD OF
YOUR OWN MIND.

Kahlil Gibran

TREAT PEOPLE AS IF
THEY WERE WHAT
THEY OUGHT TO BE AND
YOU'LL HELP THEM TO
BECOME WHAT THEY ARE
CAPABLE OF BECOMING.

Johann Wolfgang von Goethe

WHAT A TEACHER WRITES
ON THE BLACKBOARD OF
LIFE CAN NEVER
BE ERASED.

Anonymous

THEY MAY FORGET
WHAT YOU SAID —
BUT THEY WILL NEVER
FORGET HOW YOU
MADE THEM FEEL.

Carl W. Buehner

Meet Esme!

Our feathered friend Esme loves finding perfect
quotes for the perfect occasion, and is almost as
good at collecting them as she is at collecting twigs
for her nest. She's always full of joy and happiness,
singing her messages of goodwill in this series
of uplifting, heart-warming books.

Follow Esme on Twitter at **@EsmeTheBird**.

For more information about our books,
find us on Facebook at **Summersdale Publishers**
and follow us on Twitter at **@Summersdale**.

www.summersdale.com